D0455378

ALSO BY MAYA ANGELOU

I Know Why the Caged Bird Sings
Gather Together in My Name
Singin' and Swingin' and Gettin' Merry Like
  Christmas
Heart of a Woman
Just Give Me a Cool Drink of Water 'fore I Diiie
Oh Pray My Wings Are Gonna Fit Me Well
And Still I Rise

SHAKER, WHY DON'T YOU SING?

SHAKER,
WHY DON'T
YOU SING?

Maya Angelou

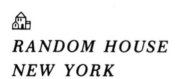

RANDOM HOUSE
NEW YORK

Library of Congress Cataloging in Publication Data
Angelou, Maya.
 Shaker, why don't you sing?
 I. Title
PS3551.N464S52   1983   811'.54   82-42807
ISBN 0-394-52144-7

Manufactured in the United States of America
98765432
First Edition

Another book for
GUY JOHNSON
and
COLIN ASHANTI MURPHY JOHNSON

Thanks to
ELEANOR TRAYLOR for her radiance
ELIZABETH PHILLIPS for her art
RUTH BECKFORD for her constancy

CONTENTS

SHAKER,
WHY DON'T
YOU SING?

AWAKING IN NEW YORK

Curtains forcing their will
against the wind,
children sleep,
exchanging dreams with
seraphim. The city
drags itself awake on
subway straps; and
I, an alarm, awake as a
rumor of war,
lay stretching into dawn,
unasked and unheeded.

A GOOD WOMAN FEELING BAD

The blues may be the life you've led
Or midnight hours in
An empty bed. But persecuting
Blues I've known
Could stalk
Like tigers, break like bone,

Pend like rope in
A gallows tree,
Make me curse
My pedigree,

Bitterness thick on
A rankling tongue,
A psalm to love that's
Left unsung,

Rivers heading north
But ending South,
Funeral music
In a going-home mouth.

All riddles are blues,
And all blues are sad,
And I'm only mentioning
Some blues I've had.

THE HEALTH-FOOD DINER

No sprouted wheat and soya shoots
And Brussels in a cake,
Carrot straw and spinach raw,
(Today, I need a steak).

Not thick brown rice and rice pilau
Or mushrooms creamed on toast,
Turnips mashed and parsnips hashed,
(I'm dreaming of a roast).

Health-food folks around the world
Are thinned by anxious zeal,
They look for help in seafood kelp
(I count on breaded veal).

No Smoking signs, raw mustard greens,
Zucchini by the ton,
Uncooked kale and bodies frail
Are sure to make me run

to

Loins of pork and chicken thighs
And standing rib, so prime,
Pork chops brown and fresh ground round
(I crave them all the time).

Irish stews and boiled corned beef
and hot dogs by the scores,
or any place that saves a space
For smoking carnivores.

A GEORGIA SONG

We swallow the odors of Southern cities,
Fat back boiled to submission,
Tender evening poignancies of
Magnolia and the great green
Smell of fresh sweat.
In Southern fields,
The sound of distant
Feet running, or dancing,
And the liquid notes of
Sorrow songs,
Waltzes, screams and
French quadrilles float over
The loam of Georgia.

Sing me to sleep, Savannah.

Clocks run down in Tara's halls and dusty
Flags droop their unbearable
Sadness.

Remember our days, Susannah.

Oh, the blood-red clay,
Wet still with ancient
Wrongs, and Abenaa
Singing her Creole airs to
Macon.
We long, dazed, for winter evenings
And a whitened moon,
And the snap of controllable fires.

Cry for our souls, Augusta.

We need a wind to strike
Sharply, as the thought of love
Betrayed can stop the heart.
An absence of tactile
Romance, no lips offering
Succulence, nor eyes
Rolling, disconnected from
A Sambo face.

Dare us new dreams, Columbus.

A cool new moon, a
Winter's night, calm blood,
Sluggish, moving only
Out of habit, we need
Peace.

Oh Atlanta, oh deep, and
Once lost city,

Chant for us a new song. A song
Of Southern peace.

UNMEASURED TEMPO

The sun rises at midday.
Nubile breasts sag to waistlines while
young loins grow dull,
so late.
Dreams are petted, like
cherished lap dogs
misunderstood and loved
too well.

Much knowledge
wrinkles the cerebellum,
but little informs.
Leaps are
made into narrow mincings.
Great desires strain
into petty wishes.
You did arrive, smiling,
but too late.

AMOEBAEAN FOR DADDY

I was a pretty baby.
White folks used to stop
My mother
Just to look at me.
(All black babies
Are Cute). Mother called me
Bootsie and Daddy said . . .
(Nobody listened to him).

On the Union Pacific, a
Dining-car waiter, bowing and scraping,
Momma told him to
Stand up straight, he shamed her
In the big house
(Bought from tips) in front of her
Nice club ladies.

His short legs were always
Half bent. He could have posed as
The Black jockey Mother found
And put on the lawn.
He sat silent when
We ate from the good railroad china

And stolen silver spoons.
Furniture crowded our
Lonely house.

But I was young and played
In the evenings under a blanket of
Licorice sky. When Daddy came home
(I might be forgiven) that last night,
I had been running in the
Big back yard and
Stood sweating above the tired old man,
Panting like a young horse,
Impatient with his lingering. He said
"All I ever asked, all I ever asked, all I ever—"
Daddy, you should have died
Long before I was a
Pretty baby, and white
Folks used to stop
Just to look at me.

RECOVERY

for Dugald

A last love,
proper in conclusion,
should snip the wings
forbidding further flight.

But I, now,
reft of that confusion,
am lifted up
and speeding toward the light.

IMPECCABLE CONCEPTION

I met a Lady Poet
who took for inspiration
colored birds, and whispered words,
a lover's hesitation.

A falling leaf could stir her.
A wilting, dying rose
would make her write, both day and night,
the most rewarding prose.

She'd find a hidden meaning
in every pair of pants,
then hurry home to be alone
and write about romance.

CAGED BIRD

A free bird leaps
on the back of the wind
and floats downstream
till the current ends
and dips his wing
in the orange sun rays
and dares to claim the sky.

But a bird that stalks
down his narrow cage
can seldom see through
his bars of rage
his wings are clipped and
his feet are tied
so he opens his throat to sing.

The caged bird sings
with a fearful trill
of things unknown
but longed for still
and his tune is heard
on the distant hill

for the caged bird
sings of freedom.

The free bird thinks of another breeze
and the trade winds soft through the sighing trees
and the fat worms waiting on a dawn-bright lawn
and he names the sky his own.

But a caged bird stands on the grave of dreams
his shadow shouts on a nightmare scream
his wings are clipped and his feet are tied
so he opens his throat to sing.

The caged bird sings
with a fearful trill
of things unknown
but longed for still
and his tune is heard
on the distant hill
for the caged bird
sings of freedom.

AVEC MERCI, MOTHER

From her perch of beauty
posing lofty,
Sustained upon the plaudits
of the crowd,

She praises all who kneel and
whispers softly,
"A genuflection's better
with head bowed."

Among the mass of people
who adore her
A solitary figure
holds her eyes.

His salty tears invoke
her sweet reaction,
"He's so much like his daddy
when he cries."

ARRIVAL

Angels gather.
The rush of mad air
cyclones through.
Wing tips brush the
hair, a million
strands
stand; waving black anemones.
Hosannahs crush the
shell's ear tender, and
tremble
down clattering
to the floor.
Harps sound,
undulate their
sensuous meanings.
Hallelujah! Hallelujah!
You
beyond the door.

A PLAGUED JOURNEY

There is no warning rattle at the door
nor heavy feet to stomp the foyer boards.
safe in the dark prison, I know that
light slides over
the fingered work of a toothless
woman in Pakistan.
Happy prints of
an invisible time are illumined.
My mouth agape
rejects the solid air and
lungs hold. The invader takes
direction and
seeps through the plaster walls.
It is at my chamber entering
the keyhole, pushing
through the padding of the door.
I cannot scream. A bone
of fear clogs my throat.
It is upon me. It is
sunrise, with Hope
its arrogant rider.
My mind, formerly quiescent
in its snug encasement, is strained

to look upon their rapturous visages,
to let them enter even into me.
I am forced
outside myself to
mount the light and ride joined with Hope.

Through all the bright hours
I cling to expectation, until
darkness comes to reclaim me
as its own. Hope fades, day is gone
into its irredeemable place
and I am thrown back into the familiar
bonds of disconsolation.
Gloom crawls around
lapping lasciviously
between my toes, at my ankles,
and it sucks the strands of my
hair. It forgives my heady
fling with Hope. I am
joined again into its
greedy arms.

STARVATION

Hurray! Hurry!
Come through the keyhole.
Don't mind the rotting
sashes, pass into the windows.
Come, good news.

I'm holding my apron to
catch your plumpness.
The largest pot shines
with happiness. The slack
walls of my purse, pulsing
pudenda, await you with
a new bride's longing.
The bread bin gapes and
the oven holds its cold
breath.
Hurry up! Hurry down!
Good tidings. Don't wait
out my misery. Do not play
coy with my longing.

Hunger has grown old and
ugly with me. We hate from

too much knowing. Come.
Press out this sour beast which
fills the bellies of my children
and laughs at each eviction notice.
Come!

CONTEMPORARY ANNOUNCEMENT

Ring the big bells,
cook the cow,
put on your silver locket.
The landlord is knocking at the door
and I've got the rent in my pocket.

Douse the lights,
Hold your breath,
take my heart in your hand.
I lost my job two weeks ago
and rent day's here again.

PRELUDE TO A PARTING

Beside you, prone,
my naked skin finds
fault in touching.
Yet it is you
who draws away.
The tacit fact is:
the awful fear of losing
is not enough to cause
a fleeing love
to stay.

MARTIAL CHOREOGRAPH

Hello young sailor.
You are betrayed and
do not know the dance of death.
Dandy warrior, swaying to
Rick James on your
stereo, you do not hear the
bleat of triumphant war, its
roar is not in
your ears, filled with Stevie Wonder.

"Show me how to do like you.
Show me how to do it."

You will be surprised that
trees grunt when torn from
their root sockets to fandango into dust,
and exploding bombs force a lively Lindy
on grasses and frail bodies.

Go galloping on, bopping,
in the airport, young sailor.
Your body, virgin
still, has not swung the bloody buck and wing.

Manhood is a newly delivered
message. Your eyes,
rampant as an open city,
have not yet seen life steal from
limbs outstretched and trembling
like the arms of dancers
and dying swans.

TO A SUITOR

If you are Black and for me,
press steady, as the weight
of night. And I will show
cascades of brilliance, astrally.

If you are Black and constant,
descend importantly,
as ritual, and I will arch
a crescent moon, naturally.

INSOMNIAC

There are some nights when
sleep plays coy,
aloof and disdainful.
And all the wiles
that I employ to win
its service to my side
are useless as wounded pride,
and much more painful.

WEEKEND GLORY

Some dichty folks
don't know the facts,
posin' and preenin'
and puttin' on acts,
stretchin' their necks
and strainin' their backs.

They move into condos
up over the ranks,
pawn their souls
to the local banks.
Buying big cars
they can't afford,
ridin' around town
actin' bored.

If they want to learn how to live life right,
they ought to study me on Saturday night.

My job at the plant
ain't the biggest bet,
but I pay my bills
and stay out of debt.

I get my hair done
for my own self's sake,
so I don't have to pick
and I don't have to rake.

Take the church money out
and head cross town
to my friend girl's house
where we plan our round.
We meet our men and go to a joint
where the music is blues
and to the point.

Folks write about me.
They just can't see
how I work all week
at the factory.
Then get spruced up
and laugh and dance
And turn away from worry
with sassy glance.

They accuse me of livin'
from day to day,
but who are they kiddin'?
So are they.

My life ain't heaven
but it sure ain't hell.
I'm not on top
but I call it swell
if I'm able to work
and get paid right
and have the luck to be Black
on a Saturday night.

THE LIE

Today, you threaten to leave me.
I hold curses, in my mouth,
which could flood your path, sear
bottomless chasms in your road.

I keep, behind my lips,
invectives capable of tearing
the septum from your
nostrils and the skin from your back.

Tears, copious as a spring rain,
are checked in ducts
and screams are crowded in a corner
of my throat.

You are leaving?

Aloud, I say:
I'll help you pack, but it's getting late,
I have to hurry or miss my date.
When I return, I know you'll be gone.
Do drop a line or telephone.

PRESCIENCE

Had I known that the heart
breaks slowly, dismantling itself
into unrecognizable plots of
misery,

Had I known the heart would leak,
slobbering its sap, with a vulgar
visibility, into the dressed-up
dining rooms of strangers,

Had I known that solitude could
stifle the breath, loosen the joint,
and force the tongue against the
palate,

Had I known that loneliness could
keloid, winding itself around the
body in an ominous and beautiful
cicatrix,

Had I known yet I would have loved
you, your brash and insolent beauty,
your heavy comedic face

and knowledge of sweet
delights,

But from a distance
I would have left you whole and wholly
for the delectation of those who
wanted more and cared less.

FAMILY AFFAIRS

You let down, from arched
Windows,
Over hand-cut stones of your
Cathedrals, seas of golden hair.

While I, pulled by dusty braids,
Left furrows in the
Sands of African beaches.

Princes and commoners
Climbed over waves to reach
Your vaulted boudoirs,

As the sun, capriciously,
Struck silver fire from waiting
Chains, where I was bound.

My screams never reached
The rare tower where you
Lay, birthing masters for
My sons, and for my
Daughters, a swarm of

Unclean badgers, to consume
Their history.

Tired now of pedestal existence
For fear of flying
And vertigo, you descend
And step lightly over
My centuries of horror
And take my hand,

Smiling call me
     Sister.

Sister, accept
That I must wait a
While. Allow an age
Of dust to fill
Ruts left on my
Beach in Africa.

CHANGES

Fickle comfort steals away
What it knows
It will not say
What it can
It will not do
It flies from me
To humor you.

Capricious peace will not bind
The severed nerves
The jagged mind
The shattered dream
The loveless sleep
It frolics now
Within your keep.

Confidence, that popinjay,
Is planning now
To slip away
Look fast
It's fading rapidly
Tomorrow it returns to me.

BRIEF INNOCENCE

Dawn offers
innocence to a half-mad city.

The axe-keen
intent of all our
days for this brief
moment lies soft, nuzzling
the breast of morning,
crooning, still sleep-besotted,
of childish pranks with
angels.

THE LAST DECISION

The print is too small, distressing me.
Wavering black things on the page.
Wriggling polliwogs all about.
I know it's my age.
I'll have to give up reading.

The food is too rich, revolting me.
I swallow it hot or force it down cold,
and wait all day as it sits in my throat.
Tired as I am, I know I've grown old.
I'll have to give up eating.

My children's concerns are tiring me.
They stand at my bed and move their lips,
and I cannot hear one single word.
I'd rather give up listening.

Life is too busy, wearying me.
Questions and answers and heavy thought.
I've subtracted and added and multiplied,
and all my figuring has come to naught.
Today I'll give up living.

SLAVE COFFLE

Just Beyond my reaching,
    an itch away from fingers,
    was the river bed
    and the high road home.

Now Beneath my walking,
    solid down to China,
    all the earth is horror
    and the dark night long.

Then Before the dawning,
    bright as grinning demons,
    came the fearful knowledge
    that my life was gone.

SHAKER, WHY DON'T YOU SING?

Evicted from sleep's mute palace,
I wait in silence
for the bridal croon;
your legs rubbing insistent
rhythm against my thighs,
your breast moaning
a canticle in my hair.
But the solemn moments,
unuttering, pass in
unaccompanied procession.
You, whose chanteys hummed
my life alive, have withdrawn
your music and lean inaudibly
on the quiet slope of memory.

O Shaker, why don't you sing?

In the night noisome with
street cries and the triumph

of amorous insects, I focus beyond
those cacophonies for
the anthem of your hands and swelling chest,
for the perfect harmonies which are
your lips. Yet darkness brings
no syncopated promise. I rest somewhere
between the unsung notes of night.

Shaker, why don't you sing?

MY LIFE HAS TURNED TO BLUE

Our summer's gone,
the golden days are through.
The rosy dawns I used to
wake with you
have turned to gray,
my life has turned to blue.

The once-green lawns
glisten now with dew.
Red robin's gone,
down to the South he flew.
Left here alone,
my life has turned to blue.

I've heard the news
that winter too will pass,
that spring's a sign
that summer's due at last.
But until I see you
lying in green grass,
my life has turned to blue.

ABOUT THE AUTHOR

MAYA ANGELOU, author of the best-selling *I Know Why the Caged Bird Sings, Gather Together in My Name* and *Heart of a Woman,* has also written three collections of poetry, *Just Give Me a Cool Drink of Water 'fore I Diiie, Oh Pray My Wings Are Gonna Fit Me Well* and *And Still I Rise.* In theater, she produced, directed and starred in *Cabaret for Freedom,* in collaboration with Godfrey Cambridge, at New York's Village Gate, starred in Genet's *The Blacks* at the St. Mark's Playhouse and adapted Sophocles' *Ajax,* which premiered at the Mark Taper Forum in Los Angeles in 1974. In film and television, Maya Angelou wrote the original screenplay and musical score for the film *Georgia, Georgia,* wrote and produced a ten-part TV series on African traditions in American life and participated as a guest interviewer for the Public Broadcasting System program *Assignment America.*

In the sixties, at the request of Dr. Martin Luther King, Jr., Maya Angelou became the Northern Coordinator for the Southern Christian Leadership Conference, and in 1975 Maya Angelou received the *Ladies' Home Journal* "Woman of the Year Award" in Communications. She has received numerous honorary degrees. She was also appointed by President Carter to the Commission of International Women's Year and is on the Board of Trustees of the American Film Institute. One of the few women members of the Directors Guild, Maya Angelou is author of the television screenplays *I Know Why the Caged Bird Sings* and *The Sisters.* She is currently Reynolds Professor at Wake Forest University, Winston-Salem, North Carolina.